Other books in this series:
Golf Jokes
Golf Quotations
Teddy Bear Quotations
A Feast of After Dinner Jokes
A Portfolio of Business Jokes

Published in Great Britain in 1991 by
Exley Publications Ltd
16 Chalk Hill, Watford, Herts WD1 4BN, United Kingdom
Cartoons © Bill Stott 1991. Copyright © Helen Exley 1991.
First and second printings 1991

ISBN 1-85015-261-6

A copy of the CIP data is available from the British Library on request.

Series editor: Helen Exley.
Edited by Samantha Armstrong.
Jokes by Mr. "J" and John Gurney reproduced by kind permission of
Angus and Robertson (a division of HarperCollins Publishers Ltd.)
Jokes by Gyles Brandreth reproduced by Grafton Books (a division of
HarperCollins Publishers Ltd.) Jokes from "My Lords, Ladies and
Gentlemen" reproduced by permission from Piatkus Books.
Printed and bound by Graficas Reunidas S.A., Madrid, Spain.

A ROMP OF

NAUGHTY

· J O K E S ·

Cartoons by Bill Stott

EXLEY

THE OLDER YOU ARE . . .

An old man made it shakily through the door to Joe Conforte's Mustang Ranch, outside Reno, Nevada.

The receptionist stared at him. "You gotta be in the wrong place," she exclaimed. "What are you looking for?"

"Ain't this where you allus got forty-five girls ready 'n' able?"

The receptionist looked perplexed. "Ready for what?"

"I want a girl," the old man rasped. "I wanna get laid."

"How old are you, Pop?" she asked.

"Ninety-two," he replied.

"Ninety-two? Pop, you've *had* it!"

"Oh," said the old man, a little disconcerted as his trembling fingers reached for his wallet. "How much do I owe you?"

MR "J"
from, *The World's Best Dirty Jokes*

"*QUICK DEREK! – PUT YOUR TEETH IN – I'VE COME OVER ALL AVAILABLE!*"

"Older women are best because they always think they may be doing it for the last time."

IAN FLEMING
from, *The Life of Ian Fleming*

"What is a promiscuous person – it's usually someone who is getting more sex than you are."

VICTOR LOWNES

●

One Monday morning a customer walked into Riley's pharmacy with a complaint.

"Last Friday evening you sold me a gross of condoms, but when I opened them up there were only a hundred."

Riley was apologetic. He wrapped up forty-four condoms and passed them over to his customer.

"Hope we didn't spoil your weekend."

JOHN GURNEY
from, World's Best Salesman Jokes

●

"PAGE 73? . . . AGAIN?"

"Sex is bad for one. But it's good for two."

T-SHIRT, LONDON

●

"Sex is the most fun I ever had without laughing."

WOODY ALLEN

●

"When choosing between two evils, I always like to try the one I've never tried before."

MAE WEST

●

"When I'm good I'm very very good, but when I'm bad, I'm better."

MAE WEST

●

Gerald Crozier was a New York literary agent, a notorious homosexual and an incorrigible practical joker. He had a favourite trick that he liked to use whenever he was dining at a sufficiently grand and fashionable restaurant. Gerald would wait until a beautiful woman had come into the restaurant and been escorted to her table. He would then summon the wine waiter and ask him to deliver a note to the lady's table. He would tell the wine waiter not to say who the note had come from, but to wait for a reply.

The wine waiter would then carry Gerald's note over to the lady, who would open it and read, "I know I'm only the wine waiter here, but believe me I can uncork more than bottles! If you want the lay of your life, I'm your man. How about it, honey?"

GYLES BRANDRETH
from, *The Bedside Book of Great Sexual Disasters*

●

"MR HARINGTON! REALLY!"

"DO I WANT TO SEE YOUR JANET REGER KNICKERS? CERTAINLY NOT – WE'D FREEZE TO DEATH GETTING THERE"

"A lady is one who never shows her underwear unintentionally."

LILIAN DAY

●

"When she raises her eyelids, it's as if she were taking off all her clothes."

COLLETTE
from, *Claudine and Annie*

●

"All this fussing about sleeping together. For physical pleasure I'd sooner go to my dentist any day."

EVELYN WAUGH
from, *Vile Bodies*

●

"Sex is not only a divine and beautiful activity: it's a murderous activity. People kill each other in bed. Some of the greatest crimes ever committed were committed in bed. And no weapons were used."

NORMAN MAILER

●

"Whatever else can be said about sex, it cannot be called a dignified performance."

HELEN LAWRENSON

●

"I enjoy it for what it's worth and fully intend to go on doing so for as long as anybody is interested, and when the time comes that they're not I shall be perfectly content to settle down with an apple and a good book."

NOEL COWARD

"YOU BRING OUT THE ANIMAL IN ME, DOREEN."

"HAVE YOU BEEN AT MY VANISHING CREAM?"

A little girl, upon seeing her first penis. "Mother, isn't it a blessing they don't have them on their faces?"

●

Solly, staring mournfully at his prick, intoned, "We were born together. We grew up together. We got married together. Why, oh why did you have to die before me?"

The Spectator

"A friend of mine expecting some visitors to tea one afternoon this week, popped some scones into the oven. An hour later she was just about to step into the bath when horror-stricken she remembered them. Not even stopping to grab a towel, she dashed naked downstairs into the kitchen. Her hand was on the oven handle when she heard a knock on the back-door. She was panic-stricken. For she was sure her caller was the baker who, if there was no reply, would open the door and leave the bread on the kitchen table. She darted into . . . the broom cupboard. The back door clicked open. But then, appalled, my friend heard footsteps coming across the kitchen floor toward the broom cupboard. The door opened. And there stood an astonished gasman. He had come to read the meter – which is in the cupboard. My friend blushed deeply – and then explained, 'I'm sorry – I was expecting the baker....' 'Oh!' he said. 'Sorry.' And carefully closed the door again and walked out of the house.

Letter in 'The Sunday Express'

"WHEN A COUPLE TAKE A BATH TOGETHER THEY'RE NOT
SUPPOSED TO ARGUE ABOUT WHO GETS THE TAP END."

"The important thing in acting is to be able to laugh and cry. If I have to cry, I think of my sex life. If I have to laugh, I think of my sex life."

GLENDA JACKSON

"OH COME ON – EVERYBODY'S GOT A FETISH –
MINE'S A YO-YO. . . ."

"Lovers behave far more respectably than married couples. Have you ever heard of a mistress-swapping party?"

JILLY COOPER

●

The recently married bride was perplexed when her husband announced that he had found a new position.

"What's that, honey?"

"We lie back to back."

"But, what kind of position is that?"

"You'll see. Another couple is joining us."

MR "J"

from, *Still More of The World's Best Dirty Jokes*

●

"Is sex dirty? Only if it's done right."

WOODY ALLEN

from, *Everything you always wanted to know about sex*

●

"If sex is such a natural phenomenon, how come there are so many books on how to?"

BETTE MIDLER

●

"Whoever named it necking was a poor judge of anatomy."

GROUCHO MARX

●

"I thought coq-au-vin was love in a lorry."

VICTORIA WOOD

●

"Men aren't attracted to me by my mind. They're attracted by what I don't mind."

GYPSY ROSE LEE

●

"PAGE 48 IS MISSING? BUT PAGE 47 IS A COMPLETE MYSTERY

WITHOUT IT!"

"COMING, READY OR NOT!"

A footwear salesman, staying at a hotel, took a fancy to the housemaid. He offered her $25 for an hour in his room, but she replied that she wasn't a girl like that. She said that when she did it, it was just for love. Now he'd put her off and she couldn't get passionate if she wanted to. The salesman happened to mention that he was selling shoes and had an extremely good sample pair. The girl gave in, and took the salesman upstairs where she stripped completely and lay back on the bed.

The rep got going and was surprised and delighted to find the girl very responsive. First she wrapped her right arm around him, then her left leg, then her left arm and then her right leg. Of course her enthusiasm must have been due to his skill as a lover.

"I thought you said you couldn't get worked up," said the rep rather smugly.

"I'm not. I'm just trying on the shoes."

JOHN GURNEY
from, *The World's Best Salesman Jokes*

"OVULATION IS A BEAUTIFUL THING, ISN'T IT, GEOFFREY?"

"According to recent studies, those men who don't understand women fall into two groups: bachelors and husbands."

JACQUES LANGUIRAND

MEN VS WOMEN . . .

"Men play the game; women know the score."

ROGER WODDIS

●

"After a man finds out the woman is no angel, he tries to ascertain to what extent she isn't."

MARGARET BLACKWOOD
from, *The Monstrous Regiment*

"I have to find a girl attractive or it's like trying to start a car without an ignition key."

JONATHON AITKEN

BUT IS IT LEGAL?

"It doesn't matter what you do in the bedroom as long as you don't do it in the street and frighten the horses."

MRS. PATRICK CAMPBELL

●

"All the things I like doing are either immoral, illegal, or fattening."

ALEXANDER WOOLLCUT

●

"You've actually been a prostitute?"
"Yeah, but it was boring. The sex was all right but they kept wanting you to talk to them."

VICTORIA WOOD
from 'Up to you, Porky'

●

"BONDAGE IS ALL VERY WELL, BUT BY THE TIME WE'RE READY I'VE
GONE OFF THE BOIL. . . ."

"YOU'VE NEVER BEEN KEEN ON IT IN THE MORNING,

HAVE YOU . . .?"

John took his new girl to the movies, which they both enjoyed. After the show he asked what she wanted to do. "I want to get weighed," she said.

He took her to the drugstore, where the machine said her weight was 107 pounds.

Afterwards, she pouted and sulked for the rest of the evening.

When John finally escorted her home, he tried to kiss her at the door, but she pushed him away, saying, "Go on home, I had a wowsy time."

MR "J"
from, *Still More of The World's Best Dirty Jokes*

●

Lunching with English friends at the time of her husband's reverement, Madame de Gaulle was asked what she was looking forward to in the years ahead. "A penis," she replied without hesitation. The embarrassed silence that followed was broken by the former president. "My dear, I don't think that the English pronounce the word like that, it is ' 'appiness'."

ROBERT MORLEY
from, *Book of Bricks*

A man was interviewing for a sales representative. One candidate would have been ideal for the position except that he had a disconcerting mannerism. He kept winking.

"Look here. I'd like to give you this job – you've got good references and experience. The trouble is this trick you've got of winking all the time. It might put our customers off."

"No worries," the candidate replied. "All I've got to do to get rid of it is take a couple of aspirins."

So saying he began emptying his pockets. The employer was startled to see dozens of condoms – multi-coloured ones, ribbed ones, heavy-duty varieties, and every known brand of standard condom.

"Here we are," said the rep. He swallowed two aspirins and his winking stopped at once.

"That's all very well but we couldn't hire a man who was going to be womanising all over his territory."

"Oh, I wouldn't dream of it. I'm happily married."

"Then how do you account for all these things?"

"Simple. Did you ever go into a chemist, winking all the time, and ask for a packet of aspirins?"

JOHN GURNEY
from, *The World's Best Salesman Jokes*

"THEY'VE COVERED THEMSELVES IN THE SMALL PRINT: IT SAYS –
'IF ONE OR BOTH FEET SWELL UP, CONSULT YOUR DOCTOR'."

SEXUAL SERVICES . . .

"Most of us spend the first six days of the week sowing wild oats, and then go to church on the Sunday to pray for a crop failure."

FRED ALLEN

●

"By marrying I can only make one woman happy: by remaining single I can make so many!"

FREDERICK LONSDALE

●

"My husband believes that a Casanova provides a useful social service, claiming that the best women, like Rolls-Royces, should be delivered to the customer fully run-in."

JILLY COOPER

●

"HELLO! MUMMY'S BACK – THE TRAIN WAS EARLY <u>AND</u> I REMEMBERED MY KEY!"

"FOREPLAY NEVER WAS YOUR BIG THING, WAS IT?"

A notice in the bedroom of a Italian hotel: 'Do not adjust your light hanger. If you wish to have it off the manageress will oblige you.'

●

A notice in a Spanish hotel bedroom: 'If you have any desires during the night pray ring for the chambermaid.'

●

"A kiss can be a comma, a question mark or an exclamation point. That's basic spelling that every woman ought to know."

MISTINGUETTE

●

"WOULD I LIKE A SECOND HONEYMOON?"

The director of the Scottish Tartans Museum, Dr. Michael MacDonald, was in America. An old lady fixed her gaze on his 17th-century sporran and asked, "What, exactly, do you keep in your scrotum?"

The Times, Diary 18 May 1983

"I am happy now that Charles calls on my bed-chamber less frequently than of old. As it is now I endure two calls a week and when I hear his steps outside my door I lie down on my bed, close my eyes, open my legs and think of England."

LADY ALICE HILLINGDON

"I'LL SLEEP ON IT. . . ."

"The only way to get rid of temptation is to yield to it. . . . I can resist everything but temptation."

OSCAR WILDE

●

"It was not the apple on the tree, but the pair on the ground, I believe, that caused the trouble in the garden."

M. D. O'CONNOR

●

"Don't worry about avoiding temptation – as you grow older, it starts avoiding you."

The Old Farmer's Almanac

●

"That woman speaks eighteen languages, and she can't say 'no' in any of them."

DOROTHY PARKER

●

"WE SHOW EACH OTHER RUDE PHOTOS OF OURSELVES THEN DRINK THE SCOTCH, BUT STAY FULLY CLOTHED. IT'S CALLED SAFE SEX."

An Englishman visited a brothel in Paris and on leaving, was very surprised to be handed 10,000 francs. He decided to call again the next evening and the same thing happened. On the third evening he was disappointed not to be given the francs and asked why, and was told, "We were not televising tonight".

CHRISTINA FOYLE
from, *My Lords, Ladies and Gentlemen*

"MISS PERKINS"

"If it weren't for pickpockets, I'd have no sex life at all."

RODNEY DANGERFIELD

•

"Don't knock masturbation, it's sex with someone you love."

WOODY ALLEN

•

"YES, MR. SWARBRICK?"

A rather grotesque elderly man was always seen escorting the most beautiful young lady.

On one occasion, he was asked, "Where is your sex appeal?"

To which the reply was, "In the bank".

W. B. FRASER
from, *My Lords, Ladies and Gentlemen*

●

"An erection at will is the moral equivalent of a valid credit card."

ALEX COMFORT

●

In Japan a new invention is on the market: a plastic facsimile hymen to be fitted for the bride's wedding night.

●

"DIETS ARE ALL VERY WELL, BUT THERE'S A LOT LESS OF YOU TO

LUST AFTER NOW. . . ."

"Bisexuality doubles your chance for a date on Saturday night."

WOODY ALLEN

"YOU'RE TRYING TO TELL ME SOMETHING AREN'T YOU?"

After picking up his fare an Athenian taxi-driver asked where the man wanted to go and was slightly taken aback to be given his own address. After dropping his passenger and being paid he watched with fascination as the man took out a key and let himself in through the door.

Using his own key the driver followed him and interrupted the man's secret liaison with his wife.

"It must have been his unlucky day," said the driver philosophically. "Athens has 70,000 taxis."

GYLES BRANDRETH
from, *The Bedside Book of Great Sexual Disasters*

●

"I like to wake up feeling a new man."

JEAN HARLOW

●

OUT OF THE MOUTHS . . .

Some of the replies given by a group of five-to seven-year-olds from New York State who were asked, how are babies made?:

– "Mom makes babies with Dr. Roberts. I dunno how they do it."

– " If a man and woman love each other very, very much the woman will grow a baby inside her body."

– "Dad has a carrot that he plants in Mom's cabbage patch. About a year later the baby has been grown."

– "Mom collects the babies from the hospital where they are born somehow."

– "Mom takes a pill every day and it's a baby pill. It makes a baby grow inside her tummy. When it's one year old it comes out of her and cries."

– "Mom and Dad are happy together and then a baby comes along."

"HE ALWAYS LOOKS SLIGHTLY ASHAMED OF HIMSELF

AFTERWARDS. . . ."

– "The father gives the mother plenty of money. If he gives her enough, she goes out and gets a baby."

– "To have a baby you go on a special diet and eat spinach and coal and stuff. Then you get real fat and that's the baby inside you. When you are so fat, the doctor cuts you open and gets the baby."

GYLES BRANDRETH
from, *The Bedside Book of Great Sexual Disasters*

During the Victorian age some people were so offended by the legs of the grand piano that they pulled pantaloons over them to cover their suggestive shape.

●

"NOW HEAR THIS! MR. FARNSWICK HAS JUST ASKED ME TO GO TO THE STOCKROOM WITH HIM!"

"IT'S GIVEN ME A PAY AND DISPLAY STICKER FOR 2 HOURS!"

Richard Olivier, the son of Sir Laurence Olivier and Joan Plowright, was only a little boy when, on the front at Brighton, he was confronted by the sight of two dogs mating. The lad turned to Noel Coward, who was the Oliviers' house guest, and said, "What are they doing, Uncle Noel?"

"The one in front is blind," said Coward unperturbed, "and the one behind is being very, very sweet and pushing him all the way to St Dunstan's."

GYLES BRANDRETH
from, *The Bedside Book of Great Sexual Disasters*

Three nuns were walking along the street and one was describing with her hands the tremendous grapefruit she'd seen in Florida.

The second one, also with her hands, described the huge bananas she'd seen in Jamaica.

The third nun, a little deaf, asked, "Father who?"

MR "J"
from, The World's Best Dirty Jokes

●

"Sex appeal is fifty percent what you've got and fifty percent what people think you've got."

SOPHIA LOREN

●

"However carefully you phrase the history of your sex-life, you're bound to emerge as a boaster, a braggart, a liar, or a laughing-stock."

WILLIAM RUSHTON

●

"I DON'T KNOW WHETHER I APPROVE OF TOPLESS BARMAIDS. . . ."

"DEAR AUBREY,

THANK YOU FOR YOUR LETTER WHICH ELEVATED ME TO
TRANSPORTS OF DELIGHT.

YOURS EVER, EVELYN

P.S. I BELIEVE 'NIPPLE' HAS TWO P's"

"To err is human – but it feels divine."

MAE WEST

●

A nosy neighbour remonstrated with the woman in the adjoining apartment. "Mrs Smith, do you think it right that this seventeen-year-old boy spends three hours every night in your apartment?"

Mrs Smith replied, "It's a platonic friendship. It's play for him and a tonic for me."

MR "J"

from, *Still More of The World's Best Dirty Jokes*

●

"Love is not the dying moan of a distant violin – it's the triumphant twang of a bedspring."

S. J. PERELMAN

●

"My father told me all about the birds and the bees. The liar – I went steady with a woodpecker until I was twenty-one."

BOB HOPE

"FANTASIES ARE ALL VERY WELL, BRENDA – BUT I DON'T THINK I CAN HANDLE THIS. . . ."

"LOOK! I BOUGHT THE EXTENDED VERSION OF 'NESSUN DORMA' –
NOW WE CAN MAKE IT LAST LOTS LONGER!"

The aged patient doddered into the doctor's office with a serious complaint.

"Doc, you've got to do something to lower my sex drive."

"Come on now, Mr. Peters," the doctor said, "your sex drive's all in your head."

"That's what I mean; you've got to lower it a little."

MR "J"
from, *Still More of The World's Best Dirty Jokes.*

"She gave me a smile I could feel in my hip pocket."

RAYMOND CHANDLER
from, *Farewell my Lovely*

"I WONDER IF YOU'D MIND IF I ACCUSED YOU OF SEXUAL
HARASSMENT WITHIN EARSHOT OF MY MALE COLLEAGUES?"

DOCTOR, DOCTOR . . .

Then there is the story of the eighty-year-old Italian roué who called on his doctor.

"Professore, I would like you to examine me. To see if I am sexually fit."

"Very well, let me see your sex organs, please."

The aged patient replied, "Eccoli," and stuck out his index finger and his tongue.

MR "J"
from, *The World's Best Dirty Jokes*

●

"Just as most women like male gynaecologists, I think most men like lady vasectomists. One of my most masculine patients said, 'It's sort of natural taking off your trousers in front of a woman.' "

Dr. CAROLINE DEYS
from, *The Observer*

●

WATCH OUT! HERE COME THE WOMEN . . .

"He says his lust is in his heart. I hope it's a little lower."

SHIRLEY MACLAINE

●

"Goodness, what beautiful diamonds."
"Goodness has nothing to do with it, dearie."

VINCENT LAWRENCE
from, 'Night after Night'

●

"It is possible that blondes also prefer gentlemen."

MAMIE VAN DOREN

●

"It's not the men in my life that count; it's the life in my men."

MAE WEST

"Lord give me chastity – but not yet."

SAINT AUGUSTINE